HALF-HUMAN MONSTERS

AND OTHER FIENDS

by Ruth Owen

Consultant: Troy Taylor
President of the American Ghost Society

BEARPORT
PUBLISHING

New York, New York

Credits

Cover and Title Page, © Kevin Mazur/Getty Images; 5, © Hermera/Thinkstock, © F1Online/Thinkstock, and © iStockphoto/Thinkstock; 6–7, © Lilkar/Shutterstock, © Dario Sabljak/Shutterstock, © YorkBerlin/Shutterstock, © Jeff Thrower/Shutterstock and © Bettmann/Corbis; 8–9, © BMJ/Shutterstock and © Sarah Holmlund/Shutterstock; 11T, © Randy Rimland/Shutterstock; 11B, © Vitaly Chernyshenko/Shutterstock; 12–13, © axel2001/Shutterstock; 12B, © Topical Press Agency/Getty Images; 13, © Kevin Mazur/Getty Images; 15, © Bettmann/Corbis; 16–17, © cozyta/Shutterstock, © Emma Bowring, © Yuttasak Jannarong/Shutterstock and © Madlen/Shutterstock; 18–19, © Ryan Doan; 20–21, © Jaime Chirinos/Science Photo Library; 22–23, © Alex Tomlinson; 25T, © Bettmann/Corbis; 25B, © epa/Corbis; 26–27, © Jaime Chirinos/Science Photo Library and © Peter Gudella/Shutterstock; 28L, © Dung Vo Trung/Corbis; 28R, © szpeti/Shutterstock and © Linda Bucklin/Shutterstock; 29TL, © Andrea Danti/Shutterstock; 29TR, © Linda Bucklin/Shutterstock; 29B, © Dale O'Dell/Alamy.

Publisher: Kenn Goin
Editorial Director: Adam Siegel
Creative Director: Spencer Brinker
Design: Emma Randall
Editor: Mark J. Sachner
Photo Researcher: Ruby Tuesday Books Ltd

Library of Congress Cataloging-in-Publication Data in process at time of publication (2013)
Library of Congress Control Number: 2012039962
ISBN-13: 978-1-61772-725-2 (library binding)

For more information, write to Bearport Publishing Company, Inc., 45 West 21st Street, Suite 3B, New York, New York 10010. Printed in the United States of America.

10 9 8 7 6 5 4 3 2 1

Contents

The Mothman

On a pitch-black November night in 1966, two couples, Steve and Mary Mallette and Roger and Linda Scarberry, were driving near the city of Point Pleasant, West Virginia. Suddenly, they spotted something up ahead in the road. As they got closer, their car's headlights lit up a huge, winged figure. The creature stood nearly seven feet (2 m) tall, and its large eyes glowed a fiery red.

Terrified, the friends quickly drove away from the beast, but within seconds, the creature appeared again on a nearby hillside. This time, it opened its huge, batlike wings and flew after the car. The couples sped off, driving 100 miles an hour (160 kph) to try to get away from the creature, but it easily matched their speed. The flying monster chased the car to the Point Pleasant city limits—and then vanished into thin air!

That night, several other people claimed they saw a large, winged beast around Point Pleasant. The terrifying creature became known as the Mothman.

The Lair of the Mothman

The Mallettes and the Scarberrys saw the Mothman in an area of woodland. The woods contained buildings and underground tunnels once used by the military for storing explosives. Many people believed that these abandoned buildings were the hiding place, or **lair**, of the Mothman.

5

Disaster at Silver Bridge

In the months that followed the 1966 sighting, many people in the Point Pleasant area had terrifying encounters with the **fiendish** Mothman. By the winter of 1967, however, the sightings died out. The story of the winged monster was far from over, though.

On the evening of December 15, 1967, the Silver Bridge, which connected Point Pleasant to Gallipolis, Ohio, was packed with rush-hour traffic. Out of nowhere, the bridge started shaking and then collapsed. Vehicles **plummeted** into the icy waters of the Ohio River below. Forty-six people fell to their deaths.

After the tragedy, rumors began to spread that the Mothman sightings and the bridge disaster were somehow connected. Some people wondered if the appearance of the Mothman was an **omen** that a disaster would befall the city.

Did the Mothman really exist? Was it a **supernatural** creature? Or is there a logical explanation for the sightings? To this day, there are many questions that are still unanswered.

Eyewitness Reports

Around 100 people in the Point Pleasant area reported seeing the Mothman. The witnesses all described the figure as tall with batlike wings about ten feet (3 m) across.

The Owlman of Mawnan

The people of Point Pleasant are not the only ones that have been terrorized by a huge, winged creature. On July 3, 1976, teenagers Sally Chapman and Barbara Perry had a frightening experience while camping in a dark forest near the village of Mawnan in England.

The two friends were outside their tent when they heard a strange hissing noise. As they turned toward the sound, they saw an owl-like creature as tall as a grown man. The creature had gray feathers, pointed ears, piercing red eyes, and crablike **pincers** instead of feet.

Over the years, many people have reported seeing a monstrous, birdlike creature in the Mawnan area. The terrifying half-man, half-bird monster is known as the Owlman of Mawnan.

Flying Creatures

In 1976, two sisters, June and Vicky Melling, were on vacation in Mawnan when they saw a large flying creature. The girls described it as, "a big man with flapping wings." The sisters were so terrified that they immediately left for home.

Monsters or Giant Birds?

Did the people in Point Pleasant and Mawnan really see huge, winged half-human creatures? One **theory** is that the witnesses simply saw very large birds. Some scientists suggested that the Mothman encounters were actually sightings of sandhill cranes. These large birds are about four feet (1.2 m) tall with wingspans of 6.5 feet (2 m). The birds have bright red skin on top of their heads. Could this red patch have been mistaken for glowing red eyes?

In the case of the Owlman, bird experts think the witnesses may have seen an eagle owl, which can have a wingspan of six feet (1.8 m). In the dark forest, could a large owl have been mistaken for some kind of monster?

The terrified people who encountered the Mothman and Owlman feel sure that what they saw was not a bird. They think it was an unexplained, supernatural creature.

Owlman or Owl?

Witnesses Sally Chapman and Barbara Perry described the Owlman as having pincers like a crab. All owls have two front-facing and two backward-facing claws on each foot. Did the girls simply see a very large owl with clawed feet?

An owl's claws

Could a sandhill crane in flight be mistaken for a giant half-human, half-moth creature?

A Mountain Monster

In the Himalaya Mountains in Asia, people have believed in the existence of a giant, half-human creature for centuries. The yeti is a hairy, apelike beast that walks upright on two legs. One woman from Nepal claims to have had an up-close encounter with a yeti.

The horrifying experience took place in 1974. Lhakpa Dolma was **herding** her **yaks** on a remote mountain slope. As she cared for her animals, she suddenly felt the ground shuddering. Then, a powerful creature grabbed her from behind and tossed her into a stream. The creature killed three of her yaks before disappearing. There were no other witnesses to the attack, but Lhakpa was certain the beast was a yeti.

Yeti Footprints

In 1951, British mountaineer Eric Shipton discovered footprints on a snowy mountain slope high in the Himalayas. Each footprint was about 18 inches (46 cm) long. Could the giant tracks have been made by a yeti?

Is this a yeti's footprint?

The Mysterious Bigfoot

The yeti is not the only apelike creature said to roam Earth. Many people believe in the existence of another giant, hairy creature that walks on two legs—Bigfoot.

Also known as Sasquatch, this type of creature lives in dense forests and remote mountains. Bigfoots have been spotted in almost every state in the United States and also in Canada. Since the early 1950s, investigators have collected thousands of Bigfoot reports. These include sightings of the creatures and discoveries of giant footprints.

On October 20, 1967, two cowboys, Roger Patterson and Robert Gimlin, saw a Bigfoot near Bluff Creek, California. Using a movie camera, Patterson filmed the creature walking. Some people believe that Patterson's short movie just shows a person in a costume. Others, however, believe the 7.5-foot (2.3 m) tall figure really is the mysterious Bigfoot.

A still from Roger Patterson's Bigfoot movie

Bigfoot Profile

This Bigfoot profile has been compiled from hundreds of reports:

- Covered with thick black, brown, reddish, or grayish-white hair
- Has very long arms with hands hanging down to its knees
- May grow to ten feet (3 m) tall
- A footprint can be up to 27 inches (68.5 cm) long
- Gives off a strong, horrible smell

Do Yetis and Bigfoots Exist?

Are the yeti and Bigfoot real? Eyewitnesses, scientists, and investigators have been arguing about this mystery for years. Some people are certain that the sightings of these beasts are made up. Others, however, think that people have mistaken an actual animal, such as a bear, for the mysterious monsters.

Still others believe that the yeti and Bigfoot are relatives of a huge, prehistoric ape called *Gigantopithecus* (jeye-*gan*-toh-PITH-uh-cuhs). This cousin of the orangutan stood eight to ten feet (2.4 to 3 m) tall and lived on Earth for millions of years. *Gigantopithecus* is believed to have become **extinct** about 100,000 years ago. Is it possible, however, that some of these giant apes survived? Are modern-day relatives of a prehistoric creature living and **breeding** in the Himalayas and in the forests of North America?

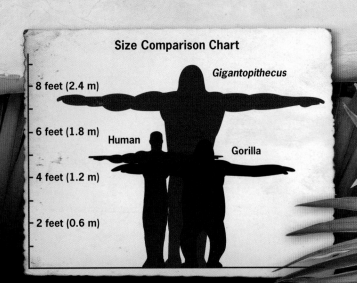

Size Comparison Chart

8 feet (2.4 m)

Gigantopithecus

6 feet (1.8 m)
Human

4 feet (1.2 m)

Gorilla

2 feet (0.6 m)

A *Gigantopithecus*

Bigfoot Bones

Some people ask why no Bigfoot bones have ever been found. Bigfoot investigators point out that people rarely find wild animal bones in a forest or wilderness area. This is because when an animal dies, its body and bones may be eaten by other animals.

A Devilish Fiend

In the dense forests of the Pine Barrens area of New Jersey, people live in fear of an unexplained creature—the Jersey Devil. According to legend, this hideous creature came into the world in 1735—the thirteenth child of a woman named Jane Leeds. At birth, the creature looked like an ordinary human baby. Then, it began to **mutate** into a monster with a horse's head, a long tail, and large, batlike wings. As soon as its **transformation** was complete, the beast flew away!

That same day, the Jersey Devil began terrorizing the people of the Pine Barrens. There were reports of children, pets, and **livestock** being snatched and carried off by the creature.

For centuries, thousands of people have reported seeing the Jersey Devil. Were all these witnesses mistaken, or does a bloodthirsty, supernatural fiend really lurk in the dark forests of the Pine Barrens?

Catching the Devil

In the early 1900s, the Philadelphia Zoo offered $10,000 to any person who could capture the Jersey Devil. In 1960, Harry Hunt, the owner of Hunt Brothers Circus, said he would pay a $100,000 reward to anyone who could bring him the creature.

Attack of the Chupacabra

Eight sheep lay dead on a farm. The animals' throats showed bite marks and all of the blood had been sucked from their bodies. So began the reign of terror of the creature known as the chupacabra, or goat sucker. Since those first killings in Puerto Rico in March 1995, attacks on livestock have occurred in many other countries.

Horrified eyewitnesses say chupacabras look like large, hairless dogs with scaly, lizard-like skin. They have red, bulging eyes, long fangs, and a ridge of spines along their backs.

The chupacabra kills farm animals at night, leaving only a bite mark on the neck of its victim. Is the chupacabra simply a wild dog? Or is this terrifying creature supernatural?

A Mangy Dog?

Many people have tried to solve the mystery of the chupacabra. One theory is that chupacabras could be coyotes with mange, a terrible skin disease. Mange is caused by tiny animals called mites that burrow into an animal's skin. The mites can cause an animal's fur to fall out and its skin to become thick and leathery.

The Mongolian Death Worm

Perhaps one of the most horrifying creatures of all is a beast that lives in Mongolia's Gobi Desert. This creature attacks without warning, killing people and animals for food. It is known as the Mongolian death worm.

For hundreds of years, tribes that live in the desert have told stories of giant killer worms. They say the creatures can grow to be ten feet (3 m) long, and their red bodies are as thick as a man's arm.

A Mongolian death worm burrows into the desert sand. Then, when a person or animal comes close, it rears up out of the sand and attacks. The creature shoots a bolt of electricity at its **prey** to stun it. Then the worm finishes the kill by spraying its victim with burning acid.

Victims of the Death Worm

No one has ever caught or photographed a Mongolian death worm. Desert tribes tell stories, however, of hunting parties of five or six men who traveled across the desert to find food. Only two or three men returned. The lost hunters had become a death worm's meal!

A World of Cryptids

Throughout history, many thousands of people have believed in creatures such as the Mongolian death worm, Bigfoot, or the Mothman. The study of these beasts is called **cryptozoology**, and the creatures are known as **cryptids**.

When there's a report of a cryptid sighting, a **cryptozoologist** interviews the witnesses about what they saw. The investigator might also visit the place where the creature was seen to look for hair, footprints, or other clues.

Often, the investigator finds evidence, such as a bear's footprints, that proves that the witness saw a known animal. Sometimes, however, there is no explanation. Then the investigation must continue.

Studying Hidden Animals

The word *cryptozoology* comes from the Greek word *krypto*, which means "hidden or unknown," and the word *zoology*, which is the scientific study of animals.

Bigfoot investigator Dr. Grover Krantz is shown here holding plaster casts of giant footprints that he believed were made by a Bigfoot in Washington State.

Russian scientist and explorer Serghiei Semionov examines a large, hairy leg bone discovered in Russia in 2004. The bone does not belong to a known animal.

The Search for Answers

Cryptozoologists strongly believe that one day they will capture a live cryptid, such as Bigfoot. They often compare their investigations to the search for the giant panda. In 1869, people in Europe first heard stories about large black-and-white bearlike creatures. It took over 60 years, however, for explorers to capture a live one in the dense forests of China. The creature they found is what we now know as the giant panda. Investigators have been searching for Bigfoot for around 60 years. Perhaps a discovery may happen in the near future.

Many people believe that mysterious, unknown beasts could easily hide in dense jungles, deep oceans, and other unexplored places on Earth. Maybe one day soon, a strange new creature will be found. Will it be a new type of animal? Or will it be something terrifying and not near normal?

Caddy is a dinosaur-like sea monster that many people believe lives in the Pacific Ocean off the coast of North America.

Giant squid

School bus

Sea Monster or Giant Squid?

For centuries, sailors told stories of the Kraken—a huge sea monster that attacked ships with its long tentacles. It's possible those stories started when sailors saw giant squid. These massive, deep-sea animals have eight long tentacles and can grow to the length of a school bus.

Cryptids Around the World

Here are profiles of famous cryptids from around the world. Check out who's who in the world of half-human monsters and other fiends, and find out where not to go swimming, hiking, and camping!

The Loch Ness Monster (Nessie)

Location: A lake called Loch Ness in Scotland

Description: Nessie has been described as a 30-foot (9 m) long sea serpent. It has a six-foot (1.8 m) long neck and a small head.

Monster behavior: Nessie spends most of its time deep underwater. Occasionally, it surprises visitors by swimming with its head and neck or part of its back out of the water. The monster is very good at hiding from Nessie hunters who search the water using equipment that can detect large underwater animals.

Thunderbirds

Location: North America

Description: A huge, black bird with a wingspan of over 20 feet (6 m)—the same wingspan as a small plane!

Monster behavior: On July 25, 1977, two of these birds swooped into the backyard of ten-year-old Marlon Lowe in Lawndale, Illinois. One of the birds grabbed Marlon's shoulders with its claws and lifted him into the air. Thankfully, the creature quickly dropped the boy.

Mermaids

Location: Oceans around the world

Description: A mermaid has the upper body and head of a beautiful woman with long hair. Her lower body is a long, fishlike tail.

Monster behavior: Mermaids can sometimes be wicked creatures that pretend to be drowning women. If a sailor leaps from his ship to help her, the mermaid drags him underwater to his death.

Mokele-mbembe

Location: Rivers and lakes in central Africa

Description: A dinosaur-like beast that walks on all fours. Some witnesses say it can grow up to 75 feet (23 m) long!

Monster behavior: Mokele-mbembe spends most of its time in water. There have been reports of the monster tipping over boats and then killing the people inside. The monster does not eat its victims, though, because it's a plant eater.

The Yowie

Location: Forests in Australia

Description: A Yowie is a powerful, apelike creature that walks on two feet. Yowies have been reported as being around five to ten feet (1.5 to 3 m) tall. They often give off a strong smell of urine, poop, or rotten eggs.

Monster behavior: Yowies mostly stay hidden from humans in dense forests. Sometimes, however, a curious Yowie might approach a campsite at night and hide among the trees to watch the people who are camping.

Glossary

breeding (BREED-ing) producing young

cryptids (KRIP-tids) creatures whose existence has not been proven by scientists

cryptozoologist (KRIP-toh-zoh-AH-luh-jist) a person who studies or searches for creatures whose existence has not been proven

cryptozoology (KRIP-toh-zoh-AH-luh-jee) the study of or search for creatures whose existence has not been proven

extinct (ek-STINGKT) no longer existing

fiendish (FEEN-dish) extremely cruel; having the qualities of an evil person or spirit

herding (HERD-ing) making a large group of animals move from place to place

lair (LAIR) a place where wild animals rest or make their home

livestock (LIVE-*stok*) animals, such as sheep, that are raised by people on farms or ranches

mutate (MYOO-tayt) to change in form

omen (OH-muhn) a sign or warning of good or bad events in the future

pincers (PIN-surs) the front claws of a lobster, crab, or scorpion

plummeted (PLUHM-it-id) fell quickly

prey (PRAY) an animal that is hunted for food

supernatural (*soo*-pur-NACH-ur-uhl) having to do with something that breaks the laws of nature

theory (THIHR-ee) an idea or belief based on limited information

transformation (transs-FORM-ay-shuhn) a change into something else

yaks (YAKS) large oxen with long hair and long curved horns

Bibliography

American Hauntings: www.prairieghosts.com

The Bigfoot Field Researchers Organization (BFRO): www.bfro.net

The Cryptozoologist, Loren Coleman: www.lorencoleman.com

Read More

Halls, Kelly Milner, Rick Spears, and Roxyanne Young. *Tales of the Cryptids: Mysterious Creatures That May or May Not Exist.* Minneapolis: Lerner (2006).

Pipe, Jim. *Monsters (Tales of Horror).* New York: Bearport (2007).

Townsend, John. *Bigfoot and Other Mysterious Creatures (Crabtree Contact).* New York: Crabtree (2009).

Learn More Online

To learn more about half-human monsters, visit
www.bearportpublishing.com/NotNearNormal

Index

About the Author

Ruth Owen has been developing, editing, and writing children's books for more than ten years. She lives in Cornwall, England, just minutes from the ocean. Ruth loves gardening and caring for her family of llamas.